RPM

CUSTOM CARS

The Ins and Outs of *Tuners, Hot Rods, and Other Muscle Cars*

By Sean McCollum

Consultant:
Tony Thacker
Executive Director
Wally Parks NHRA Motorsports Museum
Pomona, California

Capstone *press*®

Mankato, Minnesota

Velocity is published by Capstone Press,
151 Good Counsel Drive, P.O. Box 669, Mankato, Minnesota 56002.
www.capstonepress.com

Books published by Capstone Press are manufactured with paper
containing at least 10 percent post-consumer waste.

Library of Congress Cataloging-in-Publication Data
McCollum, Sean.
  Custom cars: the ins and outs of tuners, hot rods, and other muscle cars/
by Sean McCollum.
  p. cm. — (Velocity. RPM)
  Includes bibliographical references and index.
  Summary: "Includes information about the history and current status of custom cars,
including tuners, hot rods, and muscle cars" — Provided by publisher.
  ISBN 978-1-4296-3430-4 (library binding)
  1. Hot rods — Juvenile literature. Muscle cars — Juvenile literature. Automobiles —
Customizing — Juvenile literature. I. Title. II. Series.
TL236.3 .M43 2010
629.228 — dc22   2009002184

Editorial Credits
Mandy Robbins, editor; Ashlee Suker, designer; Jo Miller, media researcher

Photo Credits
Alamy/Richard McDowell, 28–29; Robert Kerr, cover, 24
AP Images/Jacques Brinon, 44–45
Capstone Press/Karon Dubke, 5, 13 (engine)
Corbis, 9 (bottom); Bettmann, 18–19 (background image); Ted Soqui, 34–35, 36;
    Transtock, 23 (bottom)
Corel, 4
Courtesy of the Wally Parks NHRA Motorsports Museum, 6
Getty Images Inc./Car Culture, 16–17; WireImage/Bob Riha Jr, 10 (inset)
iStockphoto/Timothy Large, 39
kimballstock/Ron Kimball, 12–13 (Oldsmobile), 14–15, 19 (inset), 20–21, 25, 32–33
The Kobal Collection/Universal/Michael Fenster, 26–27
Mark Venon, 42, 43 (both)
National Dragster/NHRA, 10–11
Newscom, 40; AFP Photo/Yoshikazu Tsuno, 38; Orange County Register/
    Mark Rightmire, 41;
Shutterstock/Andrew F. Kazmierski, 9 (top); Arlene Jean Gee, 7; John De Bord, 8;
    Michael Stokes, 23 (top); Quayside, 22; Suzanne Tucker, 30–31
Sipa Press/Sandee Pawan, 37

Design Elements
Shutterstock/Betacam; Gordan; High Leg Studio; Nicemonkey

TABLE OF CONTENTS

4   *For the Love of Cool Cars*

6   *Hot Rods: Then and Now*

12   *Cars with Muscle*

22   *Turning on to Tuners*

30   *Lowriders and Other Cool
        Custom Cars*

40   *Cool Car Culture*

Glossary *46*

Read More *47*

Internet Sites *47*

Index *48*

FOR THE LOVE OF COOL CARS

In 1963, the Beach Boys came out with a hit song called *Little Deuce Coupe.* What is a little deuce coupe? It's a slang term for one of the coolest hot rods of all time.

It was created from the 1932 Ford, which was also called the Model B. "**Deuce**" is another word for two, as the car was built in 1932. A coupe is a sporty kind of two-seat car.

When hot rodders were finished with the Model B, it looked a lot different from the original model.

Hot rodders tuned up or replaced the engine to make it more powerful.

Finishing touches might include a shiny paint job and flashy wheel rims.

Hot rodders often stripped off the side mirrors and other parts to lighten the body.

Sometimes they left the engine exposed, or added a scoop to ram air into the carburetor.

The result of all this work? A hot rod legend, remembered forever in a great song.

Americans have loved cars ever since they first appeared around 1900. For years, car lovers have customized their cars so that their vehicles stand out from the crowd. Their passion puts beauty and power on the streets.

HOT RODS: THEN AND NOW

Car clubs first appeared in the 1930s. Groups of friends would pool their money to buy a cheap used car. Crammed together in someone's garage, they would build a hot rod — a customized car of their very own.

What exactly is a hot rod? There isn't a single definition. Some people think the name is short for "hot roadster." Others think it refers to an engine's connecting rods, push rods, and other parts. Basically, hot rods are cars that are customized for performance and looks. Hot rodders often make their cars lighter. They might remove the hood, bumpers, and fenders.

The frame and body might also be "chopped and dropped." "Chopped" means the roof is lowered and the windows narrowed. "Dropped" means the frame and body are redesigned to ride lower to the ground.

1949 Mercury hot rod

Hot rodders often replace the factory engine with something more powerful. Favorite hot rod engines have included the flathead Ford V-8, the small-block Chevy V-8, and the Chrysler Hemi.

One thing hot rods have in common is that no two are exactly alike! There are curvy 1949 Mercury coupes. "T-buckets" have been shaped from old Ford Model Ts. Even boxy 1926 Chevy pickups have found new life as hot rods. Where there is imagination and a set of wheels, there is a hot rod waiting to be born.

TODAY'S RODS

Hot rodding is alive and well today. Hundreds of car shows are held each year where people show off their creations. This community of car lovers has split into three different groups.

Hot Rod

There are still hot rodders, of course. They build their cars the old-fashioned way. They look for used parts and try to match the hot rod styles of the 1940s, 1950s, and 1960s.

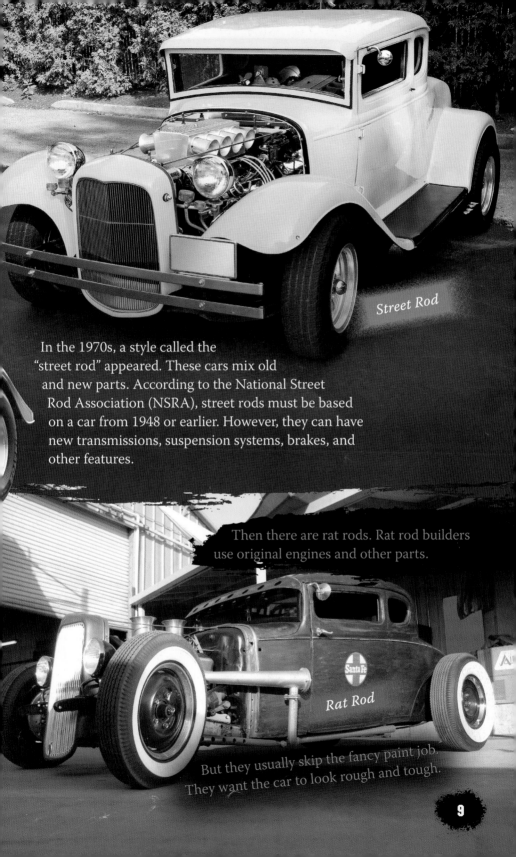

Street Rod

In the 1970s, a style called the "street rod" appeared. These cars mix old and new parts. According to the National Street Rod Association (NSRA), street rods must be based on a car from 1948 or earlier. However, they can have new transmissions, suspension systems, brakes, and other features.

Then there are rat rods. Rat rod builders use original engines and other parts.

Rat Rod

But they usually skip the fancy paint job. They want the car to look rough and tough.

RACING THE NHRA WAY

His name was Wally Parks, and he loved fast cars. He helped organize some of the first legal drag races in California. Parks later became editor of *Hot Rod Magazine*. He also founded the National Hot Rod Association (NHRA) in 1951. The Wally Parks NHRA Motorsports Museum honors the man and the cars he loved.

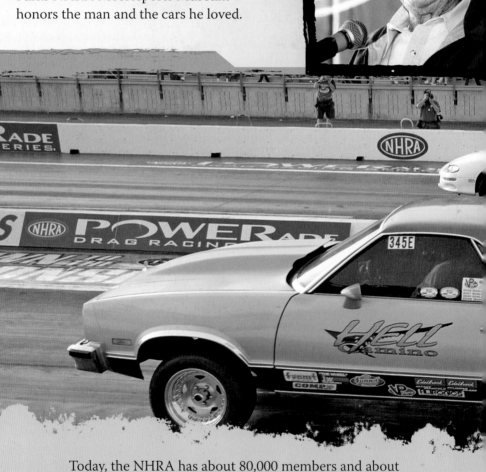

Today, the NHRA has about 80,000 members and about 140 member tracks around the United States. Thousands of events take place each year for vehicles ranging from street cars to top fuel dragsters. The NHRA works hard to provide places for people of all levels to legally enjoy the sport of drag racing.

Working on powerful, cool cars is a great pastime. Driving them in street races is not. A street race is an illegal race on a public road or highway.

In February 2008, a street race took place in Maryland. It was about 2:00 in the morning. A crowd had gathered on a quiet stretch of Route 210 to watch the race. The racers took off. The spectators wandered onto the road to watch the cars speed away.

Suddenly, two other cars appeared behind the spectators. The drivers had been racing on a different section of the highway and did not have their lights on. They slammed into the crowd, killing eight people.

According to the National Highway Traffic Safety Administration, more than 800 people were killed in street racing accidents between 2001 and 2006.

NHRA Nationals drag race

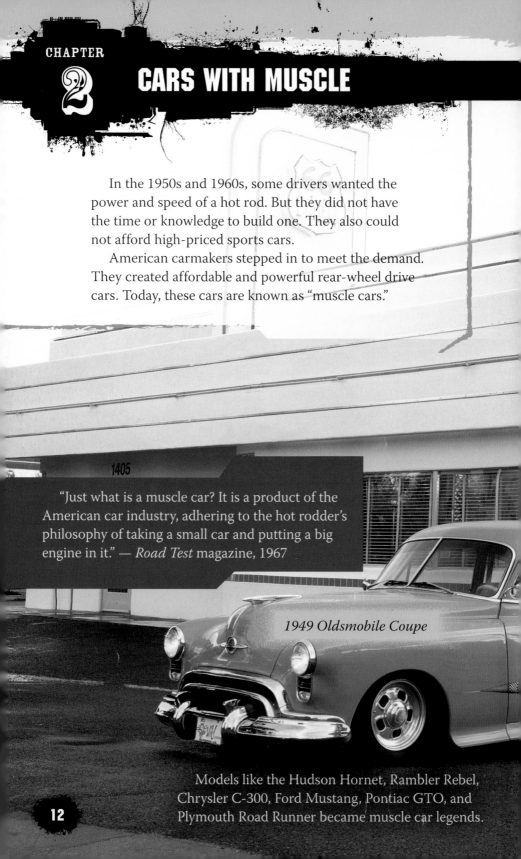

In the 1950s and 1960s, some drivers wanted the power and speed of a hot rod. But they did not have the time or knowledge to build one. They also could not afford high-priced sports cars.

American carmakers stepped in to meet the demand. They created affordable and powerful rear-wheel drive cars. Today, these cars are known as "muscle cars."

1405

"Just what is a muscle car? It is a product of the American car industry, adhering to the hot rodder's philosophy of taking a small car and putting a big engine in it." — *Road Test* magazine, 1967

1949 Oldsmobile Coupe

Models like the Hudson Hornet, Rambler Rebel, Chrysler C-300, Ford Mustang, Pontiac GTO, and Plymouth Road Runner became muscle car legends.

1955 Chevrolet small-block V-8 engine

Many car buffs point to the 1949 Oldsmobile Rocket 88 as the first muscle car. Designers dropped a big V-8 engine into a mid-size frame. This put 135 horsepower in the hands of the driver. That was a lot of power for 1949. The Oldsmobile Rocket engine won eight out of 10 NASCAR races in 1950.

The desire for more power continued through the 1950s. In 1955, Chevrolet introduced its famous small-block V-8 engine. That same year, Chrysler came out with its C-300, sporting a 300-horsepower hemi engine. It was given the title of "America's Most Powerful Car." In 1957, the American Motors' Rambler Rebel stole that title.

CLASSIC MUSCLE CARS

1951–1954: Hudson Hornet

The Hornet was a low, curvy car. With a few improvements, its six-cylinder engine could produce 210 horsepower. In 1952, the Hornet won 27 out of 34 national NASCAR events.

1953–Present: Chevrolet Corvette

The Chevrolet Corvette is the most famous American-made muscle car. Changes were made over the years to the engine and body style, but Corvettes are still an American favorite.

1955: Chrysler C-300

The C-300 was the first of a series of high-performance Chryslers. The "300" stood for the horsepower rating produced by the V-8 hemi engine. Designed as a racecar, fewer than 2,000 models were built.

1957–1960 & 1966–1967: AMC Rambler Rebel

The Rambler Rebel featured a big engine in a mid-size body. In 1957, it was faster than every American car except the Corvette.

1964–1974: Pontiac GTO

The first Pontiac GTO was billed as a high-performance street car. Pontiac planned to make only 5,000 models. But customers loved the GTO so much, Pontiac made thousands more. In 1965, GTO sales topped 75,000.

1968–1980: Plymouth Roadrunner

Named for the cartoon character, the Roadrunner was a no-frills muscle car. It was both powerful and inexpensive. To cut costs, the car had no interior carpet.

1964 Pontiac GTO

GIDDYUP 409

Chevrolet introduced the 409 big block engine in 1961. The Chevrolet 409 became an instant muscle car legend. Within two years, the 409 had been upgraded from 360 to 425 horsepower. The number "409" had to do with the size of the engine's cylinders, which were 409 cubic inches (6,702 cubic centimeters). The higher that number, the more power the engine has. The 409 even inspired the Beach Boys' 1962 hit song, "409."

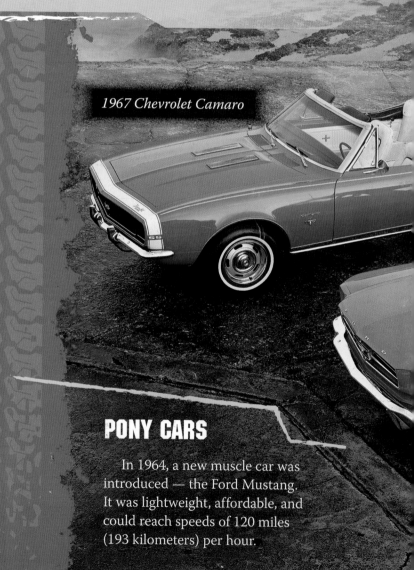

1967 Chevrolet Camaro

PONY CARS

In 1964, a new muscle car was introduced — the Ford Mustang. It was lightweight, affordable, and could reach speeds of 120 miles (193 kilometers) per hour.

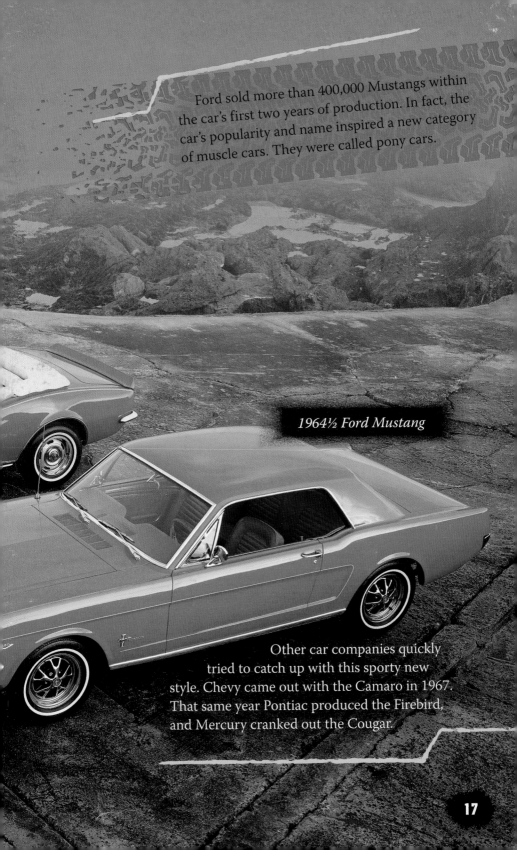

Ford sold more than 400,000 Mustangs within the car's first two years of production. In fact, the car's popularity and name inspired a new category of muscle cars. They were called pony cars.

1964½ Ford Mustang

Other car companies quickly tried to catch up with this sporty new style. Chevy came out with the Camaro in 1967. That same year Pontiac produced the Firebird, and Mercury cranked out the Cougar.

MUSCLE CARS LOSE STRENGTH

Sales of muscle cars dropped in the late 1960s and early 1970s. Carmakers began building smaller, less powerful vehicles to meet the demands of customers. Three concerns came together to drag down the popularity of muscle cars.

1. Safety

Not all muscle cars had good brakes, and the cars lacked safety features like air bags and seat belts. This unsafe combination resulted in many deadly accidents.

2. Mileage

Most muscle cars got poor gas mileage. This downfall became a big problem during the 1973 gas crisis, when fuel prices shot up.

3. Pollution

Muscle cars put out a lot of dirty exhaust fumes. A growing number of people became concerned about air pollution.

During the gas shortages of the 1970s, people waited in line for hours to fill their cars with gas.

MUSCLE CARS TODAY

Muscle cars are popular again today. Collectors pay top dollar for the classics.

There are also new versions of old classics. Ford introduced an updated 2008 Shelby Mustang. Chevy came out with a 2009 Camaro. The 2009 Hurst Hemi Challenger SRT8 with an added supercharger is said to top 500 horsepower.

2007 Chevrolet Camaro

These new muscle cars still look hot, but they are no longer cheap. The 2008 Shelby Mustang, for example, carries a $50,000 price tag. New muscle cars are also safer and create less pollution than the original models.

ELECTRIC MUSCLE

Muscle cars and roaring engines seem to go together. But carmakers are now developing electric versions of the Mustang, HST Shelby Cobra, and the futuristic Dodge Zeo. These cars are quiet because they run on batteries, not gasoline. The cars plug in to recharge their battery power.

Going electric may mean less pollution and noise, but these cars still have power. The Zeo boasts 268 horsepower and accelerates from 0 to 60 miles (97 kilometers) per hour in less than six seconds. Chrysler claims the Zeo has a range of 250 miles (402 kilometers) on a single battery charge.

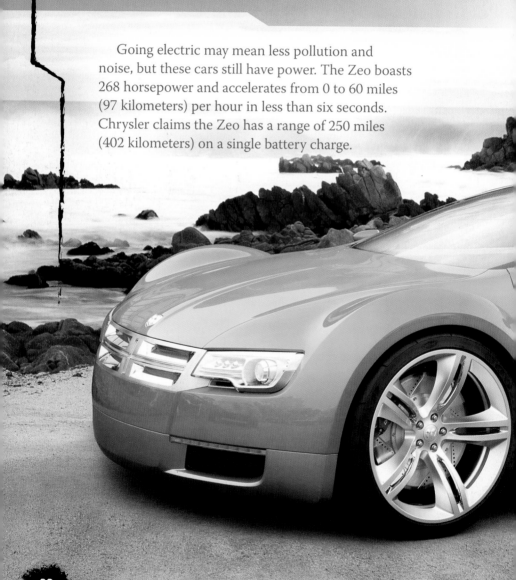

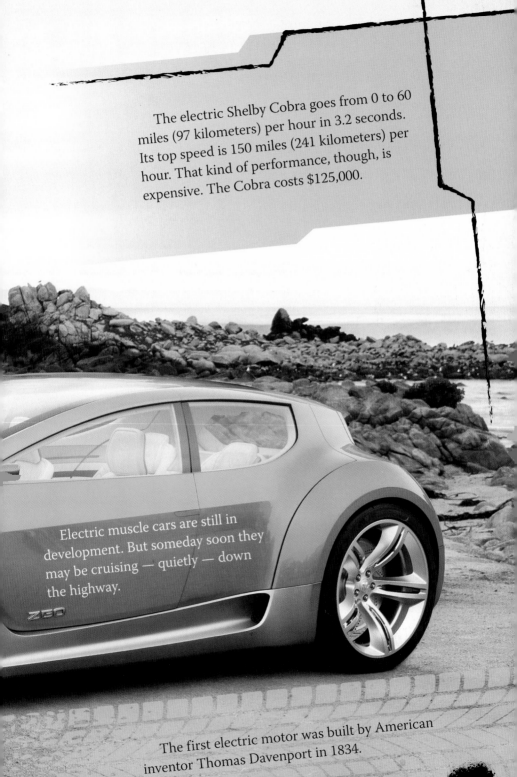

The electric Shelby Cobra goes from 0 to 60 miles (97 kilometers) per hour in 3.2 seconds. Its top speed is 150 miles (241 kilometers) per hour. That kind of performance, though, is expensive. The Cobra costs $125,000.

Electric muscle cars are still in development. But someday soon they may be cruising — quietly — down the highway.

The first electric motor was built by American inventor Thomas Davenport in 1834.

TURNING ON TO TUNERS

In the 1970s, gas prices skyrocketed. Americans began to buy small foreign cars that got better gas mileage than most American cars. Japanese cars from Toyota, Honda, and Datsun became popular among American drivers.

Like hot rodders, some foreign car owners decided to get greasy and make changes to their cars.

- They upgraded the exhaust system, transmission, and suspension.

- Owners replaced the engine or added a turbocharger for more power.

- Owners added chrome rims and sleek hubcaps for style.

- Some people tinted the windows and did custom paint jobs.

- Owners added spoilers and other body parts for looks or to cut air resistance.

- As cars became computerized, owners learned how to tweak the electronics to get the most out of their fuel systems.

These tuned up imports became known as tuner cars, or tuners. The Datsun 510 is often called the first tuner. Datsun has since switched its name to Nissan. Today, Nissans are still some of the most popular tuners.

TODAY'S TUNERS

Like hot rods, tuners are affordable vehicles that have been revved up. For their owners, these cars are demonstrations of their own mechanical and artistic creativity.

Often you hear tuners before you see them. Most are loaded with the latest sound equipment. Their powerful speakers can rattle the car's windows.

Some drivers install gaming gear in their tuner's glove compartment. Passengers can play video games while they ride.

Some of the most popular tuner cars of recent years include:

- Nissan Skyline
- Nissan 300ZX
- Infiniti G35
- Mazda RX-7 and RX-8
- Mitsubishi Eclipse
- Honda Civic Si
- Toyota Supra
- Volkswagen Golf

"Tuner car enthusiasts express themselves using their vehicles. The car is the focus of their lifestyle."
— Dick Messer, Director of the Petersen Automotive Museum in Los Angeles, California

Honda S2000

UPSET AT THE BOX OFFICE

In 2001, *The Fast and the Furious* hit movie theaters. The film featured super-hot tuners, fearless drivers, and plenty of street racing action. It was a big summer hit. Three sequels followed, as well as action-packed video games.

The movies bothered many tuner lovers. They felt the violence and illegal racing in the films made all tuner owners look reckless.

Tuner lovers have since come out with an educational program called "Tuners Against Street Racing." Organizers want to teach young drivers that tuners are a blast to build. But risking people's lives street racing is brainless.

The tuner community knows that some people want to compete with their machines. They organize legal racing events like Battle of the Imports to let tuner owners show what they've got.

The Fast and the Furious *featured many illegal and dangerous street racing scenes.*

TUNERS AND DRIFT RACING

Tuners compete in the exciting sport of drift racing. This motorsport was first introduced in Japan. Today drift races take place on tracks all over the world. In drift racing, cars slide, or drift, around corners at crazy angles.

Drifting competitions are not about crossing the finish line first. They're about style. In the first round, drivers compete one at a time.

During the first round, judges score the drivers on technique and speed.

Faster speeds earn higher scores, with extra points for driving close to the track wall.

Drivers also earn points if they get a great reaction from the crowd.

The Kumho Tire Company has developed drift tires that produce colored and scented smoke.

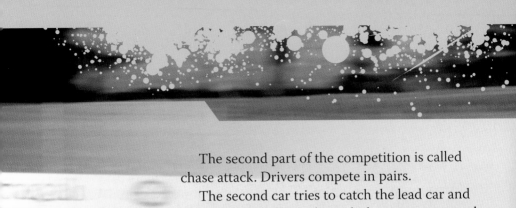

The second part of the competition is called chase attack. Drivers compete in pairs.

The second car tries to catch the lead car and pass it, while drifting through the turns at around 80 miles (129 kilometers) per hour.

Drivers get better scores when their skidding tires make large clouds of smoke.

4

LOWRIDERS AND OTHER COOL CUSTOM CARS

In the 1930s and 1940s, hot rodders were customizing cars for speed. But another style of car was developing at the same time. Mexican-Americans in southern California and parts of Texas were working on Chevrolets. Their motto was *bajito y suavecito*. That's Spanish for "low and slow." These cars became known as lowriders. They are built to look cool and turn heads.

Many lowriders have special suspension systems that make the cars hop and jump.

Dropping the car's body is what turns a car into a lowrider.
The goal is to get the chassis as close as possible to the street.
In the past, lowrider builders cut the rear springs of the suspension

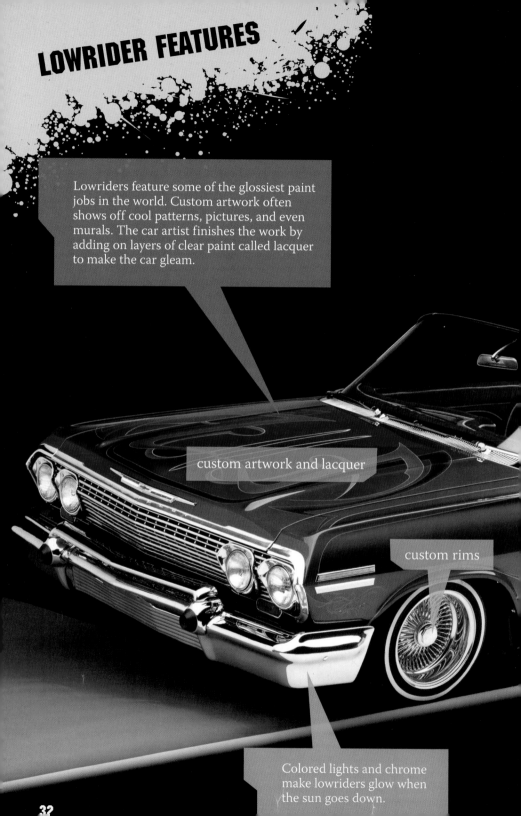

LOWRIDER FEATURES

Lowriders feature some of the glossiest paint jobs in the world. Custom artwork often shows off cool patterns, pictures, and even murals. The car artist finishes the work by adding on layers of clear paint called lacquer to make the car gleam.

custom artwork and lacquer

custom rims

Colored lights and chrome make lowriders glow when the sun goes down.

A lowrider's interior is as important as its exterior. Leather or velvet seats are popular features.

velvet interior

Powerful sound systems fill the lowrider with music. Neon lights and backseat TVs or video game consoles make the inside feel like a great place to hang out.

A BRILLIANT SOLUTION

Cruising close to the ground used to cause problems for lowrider owners. Driving too close to the ground was unsafe and illegal. Cars were always one bump away from damaging their frames. Police would stop drivers and measure the distance from the frame to the street. If it was too close, the driver might get a ticket or even have his car towed away.

This problem led to a brilliant solution. Builders added air or hydraulic suspensions to their lowriders. These systems let drivers adjust the height of the car with a flick of a switch. That way drivers could cruise "street legal" but drop low when they parked.

Many lowrider car shows feature hop and dance contests where the cars shake to the music. Pump hops are competitions to see how high a car can jump. Some cars get their front tires 6 feet (1.8 meters) off the ground or more.

THE MECHANICS OF LOWRIDER SUSPENSIONS

How do lowrider suspension systems work? Air suspensions replace a car's regular metal springs with super strong rubber bags. They are fairly cheap and easy to install.

To raise the car, these bags can be pumped up using a built-in air compressor.

They can then be deflated to lower it.

Most lowrider creators prefer hydraulic suspensions, though. These systems can be very powerful.

They raise and lower the car using fluid.

Hydraulic systems require a rack of car batteries to power the hydraulic pump.

Hydraulic suspensions are much more expensive than air suspensions. Air suspensions cost a few hundred dollars. Hydraulic suspensions cost thousands of dollars.

WACKY CUSTOM RIDES

Customizing cars knows no limits. Creative car enthusiasts have souped up hearses and ambulances. Others have made their cars look like the Batmobile or the characters from the movie *Cars*.

The Kaz Limousine looks like a spaceship on eight wheels. It runs on electricity. It also puts out an amazing 600 horsepower.

There are also "art cars." Two examples of these motorized sculptures are a toilet that rolls instead of flushes and a red high-heeled shoe on wheels.

Nature has inspired other custom designs. One Danish artist covered his Volkswagen Beetle with grass. Animal patterns like leopard spots, zebra stripes, and turtle shells also create eye-catching paint jobs.

What is the message behind these zany rides? Cars do not have to be boring machines. They can get us where we need to go with speed, safety, style, and even a laugh.

5 COOL CAR CULTURE

Do you love cars? You're not alone. You can find fans of hot rods, muscle cars, tuners, lowriders, and other custom cars all over the world.

You can start getting involved by looking for a car club. Some clubs focus on hot rods or tuners. Others are geared toward lowriders and muscle cars. But no matter the focus, club members love to get together and trade stories and advice.

Car lovers also get together at car shows. These events offer custom car enthusiasts a chance to show off their rides. Car fans are also inspired by the creativity of one another's cool cars.

Races are held on drag strips and racetracks around the country that feature hot rods, muscle cars, or tuners. These contests let you enjoy the exciting racing of impressive automobiles without breaking the law.

GETTING GREASY

Do you want to learn how to build or tune your own dream machine? The best way to learn is by working with an experienced car mechanic.

If you don't know anyone you could work with, don't worry. There are schools where you can learn from teachers who are skilled mechanics. The Hot Rod Institute in Rapid City, South Dakota, is a great example. There, you can learn everything from custom painting to engine wiring.

Some community colleges also offer classes on building custom cars. Students at Green River Community College in Auburn, Washington, work on cars. Then they race them at the Pacific Raceways track. This college even sponsors high school drag races each year. These contests let high school students test out their own hot cars and racing abilities on the track.

Building your own hot rod or tuner at schools like these is just the beginning. You can also learn skills to help you get jobs working on cars in the future.

THE FUTURE OF COOL CARS

Car culture is always changing. Hot rodders took old cars and transformed them into speedsters. Hot rods inspired future car lovers to create street rods and rat rods.

Lowrider lovers poured their hearts into creating works of rolling art.

Muscle cars pushed high-performance engines to new levels.

And tuners created a whole new class of cool cars.

What will come next? Will it be a new generation of high-powered electric vehicles? Will it be custom paint jobs that change color with the punch of a button? Will it be a new kind of suspension that lets cars float on air?

As long as there are machines with four wheels, **car lovers** will be dreaming **up new ideas.** A new **generation of cool custom** cars **is always right around** the next **street** corner.

GLOSSARY

air compressor (AIR kuhm-PRESS-uhr) — a device that takes in air and forces it out at a higher pressure

chassis (CHA-see) — the frame, wheels, axles, and parts that hold the engine of a car

customize (KUHS-tuh-myz) — to change a vehicle according to the owner's needs and tastes

cylinder (SI-luhn-duhr) — a hollow chamber in an engine in which fuel burns to create power

drag race (DRAG RAYSS) — a race in which two cars begin at a standstill and drive in a straight line at high speeds for a short distance

exhaust (ig-ZAWST) — the waste gases produced by a car's engine

horsepower (HORSS-pou-ur) — a unit for measuring engine power

hot rodder (HOT ROD-uhr) — someone who customizes cars from the 1930s, 1940s, 1950s, and 1960s with original parts

hydraulic (hye-DRAW-lik) — something that works on power created by liquid being forced under pressure through pipes

suspension (suh-SPEN-shuhn) — the system of springs and shock absorbers that absorbs a car's up-and-down movements

transmission (trans-MISH-uhn) — the series of gears that send power from the engine to the wheels

READ MORE

Bailey, Katharine. *Muscle Cars.* Automania! New York: Crabtree, 2007.

Braun, Eric. *Hot Rods.* Motor Mania. Minneapolis: Lerner, 2007.

Doeden, Matt. *Custom Cars.* Motor Mania. Minneapolis: Lerner, 2008.

Hammond, Richard. *Car Science.* New York: DK Publishing, 2008.

INTERNET SITES

FactHound offers a safe, fun way to find Internet sites related to this book. All of the sites on FactHound have been researched by our staff.

Here's all you do:

Visit *www.facthound.com*

FactHound will fetch the best sites for you!

INDEX

accidents, 11, 18

Battle of the Imports, 27
bodies, 5, 7, 14, 15, 23, 31
brakes, 9, 18
bumpers, 6

carburetors, 5
car clubs, 6, 40
Cars, 38
car shows, 8, 35, 41
chassis, 31

drag races, 10, 43
drifting, 28–29

electronics, 23
engines, 5, 6, 7, 9, 12, 13, 14,
    15, 16, 20, 22, 42, 44
exhaust systems, 22

The Fast and the Furious, 26–27
fenders, 6
frames, 7, 13, 34
fuel systems, 23

gaming gear, 24, 33
gas mileage, 18, 22

horsepower, 13, 14, 16, 19, 20, 38
Hot Rod Magazine, 10
hot rods, 4–9, 10, 12, 22, 24, 30,
    40–44

interiors, 15, 33

lowriders, 30–37, 40, 44

muscle cars, 12–21, 40, 41, 44

NASCAR, 13, 14
National Hot Rod Association
    (NHRA), 10
National Street Rod
    Association (NSRA), 9

paint, 5, 9, 23, 32, 42, 45
Parks, Wally, 10
pollution, 18, 19, 20

Road Test magazine, 12

safety, 18, 19, 34, 39
schools, 42–43
sound systems, 24, 33
spoilers, 23
street racing, 11, 26, 27
suspensions, 9, 22, 31, 35,
    36–37, 45

tires, 28, 29, 35
transmissions, 9, 22
tuners, 22–29, 40, 41, 43, 45

wheel rims, 5, 23, 32